THE
PEARL KING
AND OTHER POEMS

THE
PEARL KING
AND OTHER POEMS

CATHERINE
GREENWOOD

To Kyle,

Best wishes,

in poetic solidarity,

Catherine Greenwood

Brick Books

National Library of Canada Cataloguing in Publication

Greenwood, Catherine, date
    The Pearl King and other poems / Catherine Greenwood.

Poems.
ISBN 1-894078-38-1

I. Title.

PS8613.R445P43 2004   C811'.6   C2004-903123-6

We acknowledge the support of the Canada Council for the
Arts, the Government of Canada through the Book Publishing
Industry Development Program (BPIDP), and the Ontario Arts
Council for their support of our publishing program.

     Canada Council   Conseil des Arts   Canada
         for the Arts   du Canada
                                                                    ONTARIO ARTS COUNCIL
                                                                    CONSEIL DES ARTS DE L'ONTARIO

The cover images and section dividers are from a woodblock
print by Kuniyoshi, "The seawife carrying off the jewel from the
Dragon King's palace through the waves by his fishy retainers";
Victoria & Albert Museum; copyright© V&A Images.

The author photograph is by Linda Hay.

The book is set in Adobe Garamond.

Design and layout by Alan Siu.

Printed and bound by Sunville Printco Inc.

Brick Books
431 Boler Road, Box 20081
London, Ontario N6K 4G6

brick.books@sympatico.ca

For my parents

Contents

II
NORTH ATLANTIC DRIFT

III
THE ABACUS THAT COUNTS TIME

Proem: Imitation Is the Sincerest Form

I. SINCERE

"We will always call them cultured pearls," Mikimoto insisted, "but they actually will be true pearls because the minute kernel inside will be mother-of-pearl."

Flipping through a fashion magazine, I come across an advertisement with a photo of Marilyn Monroe wearing a pearl choker. The copy reads, "Mikimoto: the originator of cultured pearls, since 1893."

International gem markets in the 1920's were thrown into chaos by the advent of Japan's new pearls. Dealers fearing the devaluation of natural pearls labelled Mikimoto a charlatan and called his product a counterfeit.

"...by the insertion of too large a core, which cannot be adequately covered, the nacreous layers will be so thin that, to use a commonplace expression, the pearl will resemble nothing so much as a sugar-coated pill," predicts Louis Kornitzer in *Pearls and Men*.

Dental tools were essential to the development of nucleus implantation techniques. In a procedure called "the wrapping method," a spherical mussel-shell bead is wrapped in a piece of mantle flesh cut from a sacrificed oyster then positioned through a slit cut into the surrogate mother.

In search of the real Japan, tourists come to the seaside towns. Pretty girls who've never dived in their lives pose for photos in the "traditional" costume Mikimoto designed to conceal the nakedness of his divers. In the bars hostesses banter with busloads of drunken businessmen about how they wear nothing under the thin white cotton.

There is such a thing as an "imitation cultured pearl".

When he sailed to Japan, I asked for pearls. Before the customs officers came aboard, the crew hid their purchases to avoid paying duty, removing tags and discarding merchandise boxes, stuffing kimonos into hampers full of unwashed laundry. He set up his new stereo in the staff lounge, out in the open beside the ship's T.V. where the deckhands watched porn after shift. The string of pearls he threaded within the waistband of his work pants.

I refer to the necklace as "my pearls from Japan", I don't say, "my cultured pearls".

II. IMITATION

Leading gemologists agree that pearls cannot be synthesized, they can only be imitated.

"Roughen crystal in the urine of a young boy and powdered alum, then dip in quicksilver and woman's milk," reads a recipe for artificial pearls recorded on an Egyptian papyrus.

Thomas Edison, the Wizard of Menlo Park, creator of artificial light, told Mikimoto that he himself had attempted to synthesize pearls by provoking a chemical reaction in powdered shells. Mikimoto, visiting the elderly inventor in his laboratory, brought out his implantation tools and demonstrated the secret technique. He then presented Edison with a specimen of his art, which, after careful examination, Edison pronounced real.

At first the only way to see inside a pearl was dissection at the risk of ruining a valuable gem. Various devices were developed to detect cultured pearls passed off as naturals by unscrupulous producers.

"They'll never be able to get a culture pearl that an expert like me can't tell with half an eye," says Mr. Know-All in the story by W. Somerset Maugham.

If one does not have access to a Lucidoscope, there is always the bounce test: cultured pearls have a rapidly diminishing rate of bounce, ending in a flat thud. Natural pearls are much more rhythmical. Just follow the bouncing ball.

In search of the real Japan, I watch a simulated oyster-gathering demonstration from the viewing platform at Pearl Island. A woman wearing a clinical white suit and snood wets her mask with seawater and pulls it over her face then jumps in feet first. Seconds later she bobs to the surface and drops an oyster into a floating wooden tub. As she climbs onto the boat the wet cotton clings transparently to her skin, revealing white underwear.

When a respected New York optometrist tried to fit him with eyeglasses, Mikimoto insisted on picking his own spectacles. "These precious eyes of mine are for selecting pearls for the women of the world," he said, "there are no substitutes." A visionary sees through his own chosen lens.

After Prince Komatsu visited Mikimoto's pearl farm, he sent him a large silver cup inscribed in a facsimile of his own handwriting, "The works of men help nature."

III. OF FORM

"Genuine pearls – caused by an irritant such as a piece of shell, a snail, but probably not sand – are true accidents of nature that have a depth and luster and orient seldom found anymore," says Maurice Shire, one of the few remaining dealers of natural pearls.

From the first century B.C. to the fifteenth century, the universal belief was that pearls were formed from dew or drops of rain.

My mother says pearls are for tears.

Teardrop or pear-shaped pearls are valuable for earrings. Rounds are in demand for necklaces and therefore the most expensive. Most pearls are slightly ovoid, or egg-shaped.

"Some irregular pearls or baroques are very large, weighing an ounce or more," write George Kunz and Charles Stevenson in *The Book of the Pearl*. "These monster pearls sometimes assume odd shapes, such as clasped hands, the body of a man...."

The French naturalist and physician Guillaume Rondelet wrote treatises on marine biology and performed public dissections in his anatomy theatre at Montpellier. In 1554 he concluded that pearls are diseased concretions in the *mollusca* similar to morbid calculi in the *mammalia*.

Mikimoto enjoyed lifelong good health until he passed away at age ninety-six while suffering a gallstone attack. His wife Ume predeceased him six decades earlier when she succumbed to complications resulting from the surgical removal of one of her ovaries. Before her untimely death she bore him five children.

Some species of pearl oyster can be made to yield several harvests. A nucleus the size of the freshly harvested pearl is inserted into the existing pearl sac. If the harvested pearl is of poor shape or quality the oyster is not reseeded but killed for the shell.

Cool in my palm, the pearls roll smoothly against one another, softly clacking. Each luminous orb reflects my own face. Some bear a slight greenish cast; others are blemished by small imperfections. Near one of the drill holes through which the silk is strung, the thin coat of nacre is chipped, revealing the imported core.

"The kernel inside is real," said Mikimoto, "but we call them cultured pearls."

I
THE PEARL KING

Are there not, dear Michal,
Two points in the adventure of the diver, —
One, when a beggar he prepares to plunge;
One, when a prince he rises with his pearl?

"Paracelsus", Robert Browning

"But this Pearl King, ruling over his sea kingdom, whom I had expected to be surrounded by beautiful girls waiting on him hand and foot, and whom I had expected to find basking in the extremes of luxury to the envy of all men, lay in a simple room. This was the king I found, wearing coarse clothing and with only two diving girls, browned by the sea tides, looking after him on his sick bed."

The Pearl King: The Story of the Fabulous Mikimoto, Robert Eunson

The Diving Girls' Prayer

As the seal is strong and breathes air,
As the fish is quick and breathes water,
So make me, a mermaid strong and quick.

Bless me with abalone abundant as mushrooms,
Oysters dropping ripe as plums into my palm.
Let my births keep me ashore a few days only,
Only for a little while let labour make me rest.

Rouse the beach fire when I break from working,
Let the blaze burn weariness away.
Fill the bowl of my pipe with mellow smoke,
My cup with steaming tea.

Let the wind weary of rampage,
The rain of sorrow.
Lead me down ladders of sunlight,
Part the deep green curtain of the sea.

Send the eels to sleep deep in their tunnels,
The sharks to slumber in the far coral beds.

As sponges are weighted with water
May my lungs be laden with air.
Let the stone I ride down
To the bottom not sink me.

Let my tender on the boat above
See my basket tip on the waves like a temple bell.
When I tug the rope make my signal swing,
Make the basket ring like a soundless bell.

The difference between the real
and the cultured pearl
is simply a matter of authorship:
one must be bold enough to hold the pen.

Shell Game

In all this turning and overturning, who can tell truth from illusion?

Tate Ryuwan, "Playing Bowl-and-Bead"

I duck under a red
curtain and stumble
across a game – a huckster
deftly guiding abalone
shells in a gliding
three-hoofed shuffle,
men transformed by
the alembic of luck. They
make their best guesses,
each of them hiding
a heart hopeful, or bitter,
or as shrivelled as the pea
the shell reveals.

How the urge to master
that dance prickles
the skin, feeds the hunger
sleepless nights gnaw upon.
The dealer nods at me,
strokes his sparse beard,
and my brain crackles
with light. I need an idea
to clamp over the aimless,
half-formed thought rolling
uncontained toward me, I need
to know which shell
conceals my life.

Mermaid

The appearance is in every respect that of a natural and not an
artificial object — it is certainly no compound or combination,
as has been supposed, of ape and fish — but is either altogether
nature's handi-work, or altogether the production of art — and
if it be indeed artificial, it is the very perfection of art,
imitating nature in the closest similitude.
The Charleston Courier, January 21, 1843 on P.T. Barnum's
"FeeGee Lady".

Caught in a net of credulous longing
and displayed in a museum's glass case,
the creature embalmed here is artfully
melded monkey and fish. What lures
these gullible throngs to gaze upon
this genuine bona fide fake, out of water
a pitiful apery, fantasy gone wrong?

As if stunned by cold blood
flooding up through her mummified heart,
her head is drawn back in a permanent girn
on the taut beaded string of a spine
snipped in the middle. Hidebound,
hirsute as a coconut, her hackles bristle.
The wizened tannery paps are unmilkable
as the turned-out pockets of a tramp,
the fanned dorsal fin frayed
like a cheap paper souvenir stamped
made in Japan. The implausible
tale propelling us,
in ordinary reality, to believe...

Taxidermist's dream girl,
hybrid of myth and material at hand,

whose lactescent tears
clams have kissed into pearls,
whose kelp-girdled figure has graced
sideshow barrels then escaped
by dissolving in foam:

your skeletal fingers like splayed bamboo rakes
still comb the grey coral of our illusion.
Your empty glass eyes eternally hold
a reflection of the hapless suitor's heart.
Above your flippant tail a slot
beckons the lonely
seamen to mail their French letters home.

Riddle

Desire sways heavily, a sweaty
quilt hung out to air. Women call
from entranceways as I wander alleys
where the city hawks its secrets,
and the droll moon, leering
through chalked-over pockmarks,
mimes a song:

> *You and I, we live inside an egg,*
> *I am the white and wrap you*
> *Round with my body.*

Like a stray cat, the old geisha
melody follows me home.

Apprentice

Rooster, your keen eye
tilted like a jeweller's lens
inspects the ground
for the glitter of insects.
I'm hungry too.
Three days ago I fed you
a flawed and pitted pearl
overwrought by an oyster's zeal –
now it's time
your expertise illuminate me.

How you fought
my brilliant idea, Old Cock –
screeching curses, striking
my fingers with spurs
as I forced the coarse bead
between your beak's
curved blades. Before twisting your neck
free, you pecked my hands bloody,
then strutted off
in a white flurry of feather,
furiously churning
my pearl in your throat.

I watch you mull over our argument
as you stalk along the radish row,
grinding a neb full of grit.
You shake your wrinkled wattle
and I see that my crudity
still sticks in your craw.
By now the acid in your crop
has buffed off imperfection, taught

your dull student the beauty
that gleams beneath rough skin.
Finally the pupil is ready
to part from the Master.

Forgive me, Sensei.
I have one lesson yet
to learn from your flesh.

In ugly oysters
the best pearls grow, in plain girls
good wives are waiting.

Veiled Looking Glass

Nothing but poetry is good enough to describe some pearls. The luster of a great pearl is a half uncanny thing.

Louis Kornitzer, *Pearls and Men*

Beautiful One. If I say
Starlight on a Frosty Night, is there a glimmer
of the pearl most sought?

In charcoal, crushed clamshell, indigo, and clay,
the artists found a palette
to portray the shimmer of snow
fused to the hills in bright white layers,
or the sheen of lovers in the forbidden
spring pictures: *Mounting a Horse*, *The Butterfly*,
Two Birds with One Pair of Wings.
Each brush stroke
stoking the body's banked flame,
the way the subjects glow
as though lit by fireflies from within.

With what words would I paint you
the lambent complexions, the myriad ways
light loves them? One of faint lustre
is *Silver Clouded Moon*
— imagine a girl dulled by sorrow —
but the rare type possessing brilliance
and an inborn quickening like the onset of a blush
I call *Mercury on the Rise*,
while *Pool at Dawn*

suggests the same blue that runs
through the skin at your wrist.

Yet, like the master
who threw away his brush and bowed
before the beauty of the mountain, I cannot name
the colour of my longing, the obsidian mystery
mirrored in your eyes.

In Service to a Dream

I spend long days
manicuring the maturing
oysters: haul dripping ropes
knotted with molluscs
onto the raft, tear off clumped
seaweed and chip away barnacle
infestations, shellac the shells
to protect them from parasites.

Hoping to coax pearls
from these lumps, I kneel
stiff-necked in the heat, hallucinating:
heaped shellfish become
a creature crawling with sea lice.
I scrub her slimed feet,
paint her many toenails,
rippled and black.

The sun burns my bowed
wishful head. Salt stings
the cuts in my hands.
Out in the bay, tender
transparent shells, tiny
as babies' fingernails, are growing
on newly-spawned spats
numberless as sand grains.

Meantime I sit picking nits
from the back of the world's
biggest monkey. Stable boy
to my own ambition, endlessly
polishing the hooves of
the beast, grooming
the monstrous brood-
mare of my dream.

Pearl Farmer's Wife

In the hours of night remaining
he quietly slides the screen
shut against the moonlit beds
and crawls into ours already spent.

A miracle, that we've conceived
between us five children.
When he touches me his hands
smell of salt, of honeyed bait,

still damp with the work of sowing
flesh. I accuse him of being
in love with an oyster,
making my resentment a jest,

a small seed spit out
so it won't grow in me.

The Sea Is Not Celibate

*I owe my fine health and long life to the two pearls I have
swallowed every morning.*

Mikimoto

In the sting of the kelp whip slapping the rocks
and your ebbing desire, a virility potion:
you shrug off my hand and desiccated seahorses
course in a lather through my veins,
the apothecaries' measure of one lukewarm word
weighs a thousand grains of viper blood
stirred with a rare narwhal tusk.

See how the rabbit with pestle and mortar grinds
the culled pearls of the moon?
Her limitless pharmacy dispenses light
to men watching the lovers move
slowly on her rumpled mattress,
the amorous planets in their rut, and below,

the ocean electrified in its own aphrodisiac juice.
Tense as cables the thick eels twitch
in their sockets, clams unclench and open
under the tender strokes of starfish, while tingling anemones
part their soft mouths in purple expectation.

Turn away from me, beloved.
I'm drugged on the crushed pearls of your indifference.

When life hands you a bitter pill,
swallow a pearl of wisdom.

Red Tide
or, *Gymnodinium Mikimotoi*

I

I am seeing
the world through blood-
coloured glasses

my eyes seared
as though from staring
too long at the sun

II

the beach spreads its red
tablecloth with a scavenger's
banquet of carrion

the tide pools cup
palmfuls of blood

Ago Bay foams
at the mouth

III

a ruddy pink bloom
like the blush on a bride's face

a bride serving her king
a rich stinking chowder

her secret ingredient
his own slaughtered offspring

IV

my stubborn brain-
child brutally
bashes its head against the rocks

henna-red waves
tint its kelp-tangled locks

V

immerse a hand
and murdering
water gloves it
in slick red paint

on the small scouring
stones of the beach
the sea scrubs

like worn old linen
my ambition
my stained hands clean
of hope

VI

I will reach out my hand over the water –
the rivers, the canals, the ponds
and all of its pools –
so that they may become blood
and there shall be blood
throughout the whole land even in vessels
of wood and in vessels of stone …

struck with a rusty curse
a main artery
bursts
the ocean opens a vein

VII

another bumper year
for makers of plague

the Dragon King's sorcerers

stiffen their poison
snakes into wands
red venom swirls in the sea

how do I compete
with this   my staff flaccid
as the eel
washed up by the toxic water
a dead electric cable

powerless

Waterbaby

Morning sickness or not, I want
oysters!
Even one: an oyster's an
oyster –
one from the rocky crag at the
little inlet in Nagato Bay;
then I'll bear a son.

Folk song, collected in the *Ryojin hisho*, 1179

What I sent to the depths long ago
haunts me. Like ghosts, pallid flatfish
shadow me across the ocean floor
as I gather urchin and abalone, oysters
ripe with pearls. Overhead a tangled bed
of kelp drifts by, braids streaming. Bulbs
stare down with the featureless
faces of half-made dolls.

The life I bear heavily on land
floats weightless in me here. Little aquanaut,
caught in my womb as I'm held by the bay,
buoyed in the saline water while I work.
Blunt-finned limbs bunt against my belly,
a goldfish nosing its bowl. A baby
entering the world down here
would slip from me fluid as a squid,
learn to breathe liquid, swim
unafraid. Yet as the time nears
I worry – lest the mouth be malformed
I won't taste hare, avoid eating octopus
so the child will be born with bones.

The sack of prized creatures grows full,
pulls me deep into old superstition
where I half expect the stinging reprisal
of a jellyfish. What would it be,
to be torn from the water by a trawler's gaff,
mouth plugged with mucous and salt? Fear
that the sea in me will break
and the sharks, attentive as midwives,
remembering, rise from the dark.

Dream Thief

Moist, glaucus,
in my mother-of-pearl house,
its door tightly shut
against intruders,
I drink in a dream from the sea
          Carmen Bernos de Gasztold, "The Oyster"

I was blessed with big ears
fashioned to catch gold and I hear
you're the best interpreter in town.
The others will say I've stolen
their dreams, that I have listened,
and with my listening lured
their nestling thoughts to the porches
of my own imagination – like that old story,
where some fool prince talks too much
and his bright ideas, barely
in pinfeathers, fly off like pigeons
to roost in a pauper's head.

It was the oysters' dream
to begin with. My competitors tested
nuclei of lead, silver and gold.
While they sat like hens hatching notions,
the fox slunk in and sucked out
the yolk. I learned how to pry
those tight lips open and feed seed
like pills to guinea pigs. I've tried
every kernel of inspiration: shipwreck
coral, clay from an urn, stained glass
from a ruined church. Tooth filling, bone

marrow of unborn manatee. A potion
of powdered sturgeon scale and soap.

Every foreign body I can imagine,
and the oysters spit the pits out
faster than I can put them in,
then clamp their jaws shut
like gossips guarding a secret
against me. The neighbours
call me a fraud; say my beads,
like red berries dipped in white paint,
will reveal their false hearts in the rain.

I've endured those leering corrugated grins
long enough. Last night even the moon
in its fullness mocked me,
the mystery at its core concealed
like the mythic door into the ocean's
glistening omphalos. I lay on the raft
and cupped my hand to listen
above that rippling black skin,
the way one puts a glass to a wall
to trap the voices beyond it.

From the mute beds below, the sea's mind
dumbly echoed in my head.

I filled a bucket with a few
species of oyster and threw in
an abalone ear-shell snail for luck,
an eavesdropper to help me tap into
that undercurrent of murmured
contemplation. Back in my room,
I set the pail near and fell into bed
utterly drained. Have you ever heard
an oyster talking in its sleep?
As I lay in the dark feigning slumber
the thought grew louder. The whispered
bicker of silent dialects scraped
against the tin, a drawling glossal din.

The whole long night sweet
discordant nothings crawled like mites
inside my ears. In my stark
insomniac vigil, I heard it all:
gritty pleas, squelched
green weeping, belched out

insults to pedigree. You can see,
I'm willing to pay plenty
for this dream. If I repeat exactly
what the oysters spoke, will you translate
the answer cloaked in that obtuse silver tongue?

Help me find the mother of my pearl.

Oyster Chorus

a pair of sandals
I put myself on and sit
with soles together

⬚

a suitcase packed with nowhere
to go, I nurse my grudge

⬚

fifty-three stations
along the Tokaido –
how many pearls on a strand?

⬚

lighting the lamps of the jellyfish
— now darkness arrives

⬚

like a paper boat
floated downstream and sunk,
my hull heavy with hints

⬚

castanets' black clacking, song
begins in an empty skull

⬚

running my tongue over
words rough as raw pearls –
cutting a new tooth

❦

a head filled with thoughts
irritating as shoes full of sand

❦

when you reach
the heaviest bead on the necklace
then you're halfway there

❦

night polishing this month's pearl,
the abacus counting time

❦

the bright orb rolling
around to morning, another
bead on the string

❦

my belly full of autumn
I dreamed I swallowed the moon!

Beauty must be cultivated.
Peeling away the skin of an onion
rarely reveals a pearl.

Charm to Conjure Pearls

In a cauldron deep as a rivermouth,
fringed with Black Lips
and filled with Silver Tongues,
pour brine of Akoya, Atlantic,
and Ceylon
(invoking):

pinctada maxima
pinctada margaritifera
pinctada fucata
pinctada imbricata
pinctada radiata

use Cockscomb, parings of Pigtoe,
essence of Wartback and some Monkeyface
for ferment

cristaria plicata
pluerobema cordatum
quadrula nodulata
quadrula metanevra

unhinge and halve the extracted
symmetry of flightless Black Wings
for half pearls (double that
for whole)

pteria sterna
pteria penguin

mist collected by moonlight for white,
dew from a red-sky morning for pink,
rain from a thundercloud for grey, and for gold,
sweat from a jar full of fireflies.

Steep one full moon
in mermaid milk for lustre,

sprinkle on the beds of the intended
hosts

(thrice uttering this spell):

with the eye of a storm, I stir you
with stone of cherry, ensoul
with heartwood, quicken
with lunar halo, shape
with sun ray, burnish

in the names of your innumerable
mothers

I summon you, come
pearls, pearls
come!

A Pearl Merchant Weighs the Relative Merits of the Natural Versus the New Cultured Half-Pearl, What Jewellers Call the *Perle Bouton*, Used in Earrings and Other Flat Settings

I'd rather pay the same dough
to get my hands on
one single nice matched set
of pear-shaped *au naturels*
than blow the wad
on a hundred pairs
of those champagne-glass style jobs
packed with phoney implants.

What I'm saying,
it's not natural,
the way those things
just kind of sit there all perfect
like a couple of saint's
tits served up on a tray.

A Pearl Doctor on Surgical Technique

My specialty is skinning.
I work from the outside
in, a process of patient
reduction, revealing the perfect
hidden shape. One of my colleagues
is famous for scraping
a thousand pearls in three days,
but it's not a competition
for shearing sheep. More like peeling
the friable, interlapped layers
of an onion unforgiving as a bubble,
or shaving an eggshell
entirely smooth.

To keep my left hand lucky,
I take only cases with viable outcomes.
With a rub of pigeon-blood ruby powder
I polish the freshly-abraded
faces, bless the osseous white
dust that talcs the lacerated
tips of my gifted fingers.
To the diminisher of all
imperfection, master of flayers,
Time, I direct my prayers.
I strop my custom obsidian blade
on the darkness that nightly
pares down the moon.

Eldest Daughter

Father always insisted I'd been there
the day he and Mother
rowed to the island and found
the first half-pearls. A day of imperfect joy,
the sun's warmth slashed with gusts of wind,
our beach picnic of rice balls
garnished with dustings of sand.
Was that the time he showed me
how to open shells? The blade tip
slipped and gashed his hand,
half-filling his cupped palm
with blood. When he dipped his fist
from the dock to cleanse it,
salt water thinned the red cloud
and fresh transfusions of colour
swirled above the anemones,
the way a brush releases paint
into the bowl. I thought the aftertint
leaking from my father's veins
would stain the whole ocean. His expression
of strained calm while he watched
my mother wrap her sash around
the wound must have been shock. I don't think
I understood my father could feel pain.

Like a calligrapher
surrounded with crumpled paper,
open a thousand oysters,
find one pearl.

The Murmuring of the Sea

Suffering ennobles a man,
Enduring the oyster-shell's prison makes a pearl of a water-drop
                              Omar Khayyam, *The Ruba'iyat*

All things pass. The wisdom
of Buddha distilled
in hill monks'
voices rehearsing
the law of birth
and death, the lesson
of abundance and loss
repeated. Rain
returns to the sea.

I've heard it before
in the ocean's hushed sutra,
that chant carried along
with the leaves downstream,
repeated by rivermouth,
rushed through the rumouring channel
till it's flushed out
into the waves and splashes
like effluent on the shore.

The patter of the sky-
gods pissing on
the water. The same rain
pours on me.

Starfish

A plague
of fingersmiths,
as though the stars
had all fallen
into the sea
and become pilfering
cold purple hands,
the starfish search
among slumbering oyster beds
for the sunken reflection
of the moon, blindly
breaking the hinges
of the shells,
picking the locks
on the luminous dream.

Dear Husband: Letter Mailed to a Remote Kelp Farm in Northern Hokkaido, No Return Address

Don't come back.
We will be unable to meet
the demands of our creditors by the New Year,
so it is better

you stay away.
If they come here looking for you
I'll tell them

I don't know
where you are. The children and your mother are well.
Always remember that

I love you. Please
don't come home

                                    until next Spring.

Exile

All the ropes of kelp on this beach
      knotted together
could not equal the length of my loneliness.

Only you can pull me to the surface,
      holding the other end.

Between twins, between the face and the mirror,
similarities are flakes of snow:
however well-matched
no pearl exactly doubles another.

The Crane Wife's Tale

They seem like man and wife,
and the lady seems to be holding something
like a cloth woven of feathers,
while he has a staff or wooden sceptre
beautifully ornate.

Ezra Pound, *Nishikigi*

A young man pushing his noodle cart one night saw on the riverbank a crane concealed in moonlight among the rushes. The bird raised her elegant bill and hoarsely replied to the mournful squawk of his horn. His delight faded when he saw embedded in her down the red-feathered shaft of an arrow. He approached and drew it out. The crane waded into the river and let the current carry her off, leaving on shore one snowy plume from her wing.

The following evening as he wheeled his cart home, the young man tooted his horn by the river but no song answered his serenade. Instead a tall, stately girl appeared and begged a meal, offering as payment the fine white handkerchief hidden in her sleeve. When he learned she was a weaver, the young man took the poor girl home. She stayed and became his wife.

The young man, too, was poor, and had no money to prepare for the New Year celebration drawing near. His wife hid herself away with her loom till she emerged with a bolt of marabou silk, softer than moth wings, more luminous than the smooth inner surface of a shell. Her husband took the cloth to sell, and soon returned with an order for more. With sorrow in her strange yellow eyes she agreed, but made him promise that while she worked he would not enter her room.

Hearing the shuttle clatter through the night, her husband grew curious and peeked through a gap in the screen. There, in the hazy light, a crane preened feathers from her back and fed clumps by beak into the loom. A blizzard of down filled the room; feathers were strewn in drifts around the bird's scaly claws. Except for her black crown and a bustle of plumage on her rump, the bird was plucked naked, revealing raw bumpy skin.

The young man let out a guffaw at the absurdity of the sight. The shuttle fell silent and the crane swivelled round, fixing him in a furious gaze. In a voice hoarse as rustling reeds, she said, "Is my fabric not enough, that you need my secret too? I came to serve you, you saved my life." The man realized this creature was his wife.

In the morning the woman was human again, but her husband saw in her worn face the keen beak and eye, in her gaunt form a bony pimpled breast and legs like thin sticks of charcoal. The crane wife stood outside, looking toward the river and the sky. The young man wondered if she could still fly.

Gesture

This gem the jeweler to secure,
Sold all his store, both wool and linen,
To buy this pearl, precious, pure.

Anonymous, "Pearl"

You'd strip the skin from your wife's and children's bodies to
squander the money on your whore.

Bunraku play, The Love Suicides at Amijima

She moves tonight with the deliberated
grace of puppet theater, the doll
maneuvered smoothly through a repertoire of gestures
by black-hooded men. No hidden strings. No
pretense to conceal the manipulation.

The lantern hovers above her shoulder
like the exposed head of a master puppeteer,
that floating, detached face imbued
with all the expressiveness of an onion.
He did not ask this of her, no ventriloquist

recites her expected lines, but in the silence
between them it's understood – *I'd be glad*
to rip the nails from my fingers and toes,
to do anything which might serve my husband.
A brief hesitation, her hand

suspended before the rosewood wardrobe,
then, as if the assistant controlling her arm
suddenly squeezes his caliper,
she completes the motion, reaches in
and pulls out her best costume,

a kimono dyed with her family crest.
She drapes it on a pole, smoothes
the vermilion lining inside fawn crepe silk,
the skin of a branded animal hung to cure.
She carefully folds the cloth then wraps it, hiding

in the bundle her husband's shame, her own obligation,
and her love besides. The hunkered presence
pushes her shuffling feet forward,
the mothballed pelt of his old self-image
surrendered in her upheld arms.

Face

The most beautiful pearl is only the brilliant sarcophagus of a worm.
Professor Raphaël Dubois, *Comptes Rendus
de l'Académie des Sciences*, Vol. 133, 1901

In the beginning, little more than a narcissus
bulb. Bare, like the form for a valuable
hina doll, on its wooden stick the crude head
of sawdust and glue before the paint –
oyster shell, aged decades, then crushed
into a fixed white pigment – with delicate brushwork
the features built layer by layer.
As nacre becomes the pearl, year by year
the faintest expression lacquering
the countenance, by-product
of gesture and expectation, until it becomes
the man. As a great actor of *noh* drawing ghosts
with his whole body becomes the mask.

He watches himself touch it,
palpable, porous beneath his fingers.
Saving it. Losing it. The failure of such concepts
when the face in the mirror is
no longer his, the thin boyhood scar on his chin
somehow new, the quizzical black eyebrows false,
glued on, the smallest pockmark simulated.
How the truly fine mask will expose
the inferior actor, or pressed rice powder
the aging courtesan's crumbling beauty
as she applies, by lamplight with trembling hands,
the perfected red mouth on shrunken lips,

*year by year, the monkey's mask
revealing the monkey.*

Ume

Center of all centers, core of all cores...
                    Rainer Maria Rilke, "Buddha in Glory"

If you misread my character
and call me *Plum*, then
translate me into the stone
at the fruit's centre:
how it bore the sweet
burden of flesh
before dropping to split open
and find in the ground
a new form.

When I left this world
I did not float
with the beauty of a blossom
released from the limb
but like a shell scraped empty
sank into deepest silence.

Called by the unseasonable
voice of stone I answer now
to the name on my memorial tablet.
What marks me
is effaced by a hand
constantly polishing remembered love,

indelible lament
forever rendering me
fugitive.

The Crane Wife's Tale II

my face painted white
I enfolded my self   an origami bird
within the arranged folds of the kimono
sweat trickling beneath the obi
last time to wear long sleeves
before clipped wings

concealing from the groom
the bride's fangs and horns
my jealousy was hidden with the headband and heavy wig
the anger in my mouth smudged out with gall

(either he was fooled or
I made of him
        a dishonest man)

     ⁊

she who imagined being transformed
was once a samurai's daughter
and now shied from raising her eyes to face

the gossips of the town   self-promoted
through their spite to higher stations
the creditor's knock on the door and the pointed
glances of the neighbours

*

maybe I once wanted something but too long
lived another's dream
the years flew by dragging their wings

what ore yielded the metal
tip of the arrow
that pins me to my story?

*

the mother lode extracted
by a surgeon from my belly
I am unyoked now from my fool's
golden eggs

I am thirty-two
I have five children
and whatever else was in me
I will never sow

all those old vanities moulting away
the last feathers falling like dandruff
a rare summer snow that melts
before reaching the ground

If you are lucky
an oyster bears a perfect pearl,
a lifetime one great love.

Success

The water is dark and soft
she has no boundaries anymore
she engraphs herself there
                    Kora Rumiko, "Woman"

I want to find my way back
to that well in Kyoto, the night
I wandered blindly from the hospital into air
almost sweet with the faint unbearable
fragrance of spring, grass crunching
with frost as I turned somewhere
from the street into a temple yard.
I gripped the edge of that bottomless
shaft and listened to my sobs echo
from its cold stone walls.

I wanted to call your soul home
before it sank too far
into another realm, to throw
your name like a hook into your wake
as if I could bellow you back.
I wanted to hurl my grief
like a bomb into that hole and atomize
the emptiness. Behind my blurred reflection
grimaced a thin-lipped moon
and when I bent to yell, my tears
fell useless on the water.
Its surface returned my powerless wail.

I want to go back, find that still
quivering water and drop this pearl
into the dark epicentre of your absence,
as if it could halt the concentric

spread of loss, make time contract,
ripple inward, reverse. This pearl
I have summoned into being
at last, the long-sought goal
that fails to set the world right again,
mute triumph of a man who's devoted
his life to mastering a language
no one he loves understands.

Wife, I pray you're listening now.

From the Pillow Book of the Pearl King's Youngest Daughter, "Memories of Certain Splendid Things"

My playmates were always awed
when I showed them the room
where Father's exhibits were stored.
We would trace the shining snail track
of black pearls that marked the crack
in the replica Liberty Bell,
take turns (though we weren't allowed)
solemnly posing in King George's
crown, the ermine fringe
brushing eyelids as it settled, too big,
above our noses. On a gold-plated pole,
the great pearl-encrusted globe,
its creamy seas and bronze continents,
sparkled like a giant's lollipop.

The Imperial Pavilion was my favourite,
the huge baroque pearl at its centre
a lumpy throne. We practiced
with our dolls at being princesses,
sent them on pilgrimages to pray
at a famous five-storey temple copied to scale,
held moon-viewing parties on miniature
mother-of-pearl terraces.

Yet, after a while, what was there to do
in such castles? The platinum-clad rooms
were gloomy, dust the only snow
that ever fell. My friends soon drifted
away to play ball or help their mothers

pick kelp. Even my dolls grew
bored with the austerity, the velveteen
courtyards silent but for the mutter
of their recited conversation:

My sweet lord, if I'd known you were coming,
I'd have weeded the garden
And paved the pathway with pearls!

Why would I need all this?
A cottage overgrown by weeds
Is a pearl-stuccoed palace, if I'm with you.

They glittered for a time, our days
with those dollhouses. I'm glad
my family never lived in anything that grand.

Only Son

A pearl goes up for auction. No one has enough, so the pearl buys itself.
                                                                    Rumi

Blindly decoding the bat squeak
of dream, my father, deep
in his mind's black cavern, was an island
I could walk to when the tide went out.
He'd emerge blinking, to find
on the unpatented sands
a single strange footprint, me.
What perfections did he seek,
his eyes forever pearling
the ocean's green soul?

As a boy, I'd spend summers
hooking bullheads on a string.
Once, I pulled in a large fish and
before I could club it, small coppery fry
spilled out from a slit in the flat silver belly
and swam off under the dock,
a pink glimmer of wishes disappearing
down a bottomless well. I milked the last few
from my slimy, unexpected purse
and took them, gleaming in the bait can
like new minted coin, to my father.
He was angry I'd let the fish go.

Eventually, I realized he did not control
the weather or even the tides
of his own fortune. When his competitors
flooded the market with cheaply wrought pearls,
he bought up all the junk jewel
he could find and set up an incinerator
in Kobe's city square. Ever the magician's

unwilling apprentice, I shovelled
inferior specimens into the smoking cauldron,
while Father in bowler and black cape
laid down his bamboo wand
and juggled baseballs for the press.
These pearls, he declaimed, *are shoddy*
as cat skin and rags wrapped around stones!

Pearls don't burn
any better than bones. Sweating,
choking on the crematory smell,
while he charmed the crowd, I stoked
three hundred pounds of wasted gems and necklaces
on gasoline-soused coals. When a heavy rain
suddenly fell, dousing the limelight
glow, we were left alone
with the smouldering clinker
of a very expensive cement. Later,
when he made me sift ashes for molten
platinum clasps, it somehow felt like stealing
gold teeth from the dead.

Gallstones

Of his bones are coral made:
Those are pearls that were his eyes;
*   Nothing of him that doth fade*
But doth suffer a sea change
Into something rich and strange.

William Shakespeare, *The Tempest*

You have grown old along with me, faithful diving girls.
    Keiko, Nobuko, bring me my globe,
    I want to take, before I leave it,
    one more spin around the world.
Do you think Ume is waiting? Will she laugh at my gray hair?
    Her true face evades me, and my memories,
    like the places where I've travelled,
    now seem far away, images embossed on tin.

No rice tonight. My famous appetite deserts me,
    my strength and my bodily functions
    abandon the ancient junk I have become.
This morning I warned my lieutenants to tie down the rafts
    for the coming typhoon
but my forecasts these days fall on deaf ears.
    No one wants to hear
    what an old man has to say.

No doctors. No fortuneteller need tell me
    what this illness portends.
Slick fingers dig around in my guts.
Some creature has come to harvest nearly a century's worth
    of salt and bile, has stuck
    its blade beneath my ribs
where it twists as if to pry my stubborn bones apart
    and pluck out a life's
    accreted irritants and pleasures.
    Time's hard stones.

Polish these pitiless gems when I go, exhibit them
      in my pearl museum with the treasure
      hoarded from old empires.
No morphine now. I want to know when my soul is shucked
      free, I want to see
      if the streets of paradise are paved with jewels.
      Like little mock palaces,
my own pearls in the end were mere imitations of heaven's.
      My life was spent trying to produce beauty.
      No one enters without offering something,
      even a king needs a ransom.

Here, in this silk pocket are the pearls I've chosen
      to pay my way into heaven.
Fill my nostrils, the sockets of my eyes, place the last
      pearl like a pill upon my tongue.
      Thank you. For everything
      I am grateful, I am grateful.

Kai Awase: Shell Game II

He saw there the mark of a wound
from which he took the radiant Jewel.

Noh drama, *The Diving Girl*

To find the perfect match. A simple game:
each clam unhinged and emptied of content,
covers torn from a book. The pair of shells
painted inside with identical images,
one moment chosen to tell a whole tale.

But so many stories! Deep in the heart
of the castle, the ladies-in-waiting
turn the pieces face-up then down again,
trying to remember what's been revealed
as they talk. Their voices run together
like water over stones in the weedy
courtyard stream, upon which drowsy carp
scratch their piebald bellies. Restlessly,
Umesan bides her time amid the hum
while an aunt combs magnolia oil
through the long black train of her hair.
She holds an unmated shell. Most of the stories
are court intrigues, old romances – women
weeping into their sleeves, lovers wooing
each other through screens, scene upon scene
of nobles kneeling in polished wooden rooms.

The gossip of the older women drones on
as she studies her picture. Chipped gold leaf
glints under the lamps, two chalky circles
hinting at the legend of the diver
who stole back the jewel from the Dragon King's
palace beneath the sea. How does one know
which is heaven, which earth? The horizon

floats unanchored between two blues, no boat
or bird in the foreground to pin it down.
Viewed sideways, the white moons look like
blind eyes, or a pair of pale breasts. Umesan
shivers, a little gooseflesh thrill, imagining
ocean and chill air, the girl's bare skin at the point
where she slips between realms.

∞

This must be the moment before. Or just after.

Before the girl breaks the surface and dives
into the marriage of the moon and
its reflection, lunatic, lured by the pearl.
The rope of a thousand fathoms
knotted roughly around her waist
unspooling from the boat, umbilical;
the dagger guiding her outstretched arms
a dowsing rod, its dull pointed weight
pulling her down.

Some pact of blood
and breath directs this search
in the star-drowning dark, where she drifts
like a kite on cold currents down, through squalls
of small fish, their silvery rain pouring
from plankton cloud, around wrecks

blanketed in green smog, their masts
forlorn as fogged steeples. Obliquely,
blindly down, down through murk, past lurking
shapes that glide slow as hawks above the unlit
city of the abyss, through throngs of gelatinous
creatures combing its stony middens – odd
winged octopi and pale rubbery fishes.
All the blanched, boneless citizens
glowing like ghosts, their huge eyes bowls
begging for light. Past urchins blessing
the coral polypidoms with blizzards of milt,
and, priestly, the carapaced lobsters, anointing
flurries of larvae delicate and dense as snow.

And so, on down.
Into the frigid crevasse, her depth-drugged
blood immune to the banners of tentacles
brandishing vivid poisons; through gardens
of venomous flowers; over the sudden explosions
of mud sharks hidden in the silt.

Until the dagger in her hand quivers,
and points, as an animal's raised paw, toward
its prey: there stands the green tower, tilted
amid eddying sandstorms in sunken, desolate
splendour, its radiant cargo guarded within. Past

crocodile sentries and ramparts of breathing
rock, sluggard armies camouflaged as skulls,
until somehow she reaches its glow,
and lifts, like an egg from the nest, the pearl
cradled in the dragon's livid coils.

⬨

Umesan doesn't care about
the spoils, but the sacrifice the diver makes
to attain the exorbitant dowry. She wants
to see the dragon stir like a jilted lover,
unsheathe himself from the jade scabbard
– *three hundred feet high!* – and rise
like a terrible sword in the water,
scarlet crest and mane flowing bright as blood
down the steely blue blade of his spine.
The moment the diver, surrounded
by sting-wielding minions, tugged
by the tenuous tether of air, decides she must
conceal what she has seized. How she yields
and forces the dagger to its hilt into the flesh
that shields her heart. While above, leashed
by long seconds of fear, those who watched her
disappear into the mute, unimaginable weather
sense the slack line suddenly tighten.

But this must be after. After the wondering men
have reeled her in like wet laundry, her body

a ruined gown, the veil of blood she wore
trailing, a froth of pink flowers, gone.
As one of them, back on shore, fingers the gash
beneath her breast and frowns when he feels
the curved hardness of the gem, as though finding
a stone smuggled through the wash in a pocket.

∾

At last her turn comes and she plunges
into the scattering of down-turned pieces,
fishing for the other side of the story,
the male half of her shell: where the moon,
painted white, surrenders its twin
to the rippling untorn water, heaven's
earthly copy captured in the pearl.

While beneath the ocean's indigo skin
the dragon, aroused, circles his keep
in confusion, chin whiskers drooping
like the jowls of the emperor's spaniel
when she wearies of tossing its ball.

Or sleeps yet, curled, in his deep metal dream.

∾

Postscript: Pearl Island, a Noh Drama

Persons in order of appearance

A Tourist	*waki*
Diving Girl (white cotton *ama* costume, diving mask)	*maeshite*
The Pearl King (cape, derby hat, bamboo sceptre)	*tsure*
Diving Girl (*ama* costume, unmasked)	*nochijite*
Hostess	*ai*

PART FIRST

TOURIST   You see before you a traveller. I've heard stories of warehouses heaped with pearls:

> bowls full of white pearls glowing like rice,
> bunches of knotted strands yellow as corncobs,
> pearls blue as shimmering fish scales,
> pink as liquor distilled from the headiest sunset.

The idea alone of a pearl black as a jawbreaker makes my mouth water. Perhaps these people will tell me where to find this fabled island of pearls.

(A diving girl shivers on the beach, her costume a cold, wet caul. Her companion stands beside his sceptre, which is planted in the sand; on it, like a flag, he has hung his hat. This is a sign that he is not in his right mind. He holds an octopus, a rucked red sack weighted with seawater, its eight arms twirling in futile entreaty – even avatars have their off days.)

TOURIST   Hello, can you tell me where I might find these so-called pearls that go for a dime a dozen?

DIVING GIRL   Sleeves forever wet
　　　　　　　with the ocean's tears,
　　　　　　　I wring the sorrow
　　　　　　　from my second skin.
　　　　　　　I rely on long breaths
　　　　　　　to pull me to the bottom
　　　　　　　but today my heart alone
　　　　　　　is heavy enough to drag me down.

(Back-story sound effects: the sea stone-washing a few unmentionables, *sloshity slosh slosh*.)

TOURIST   Hmm, wonder what's going on. Excuse me, I mean ...

(Magical portal, the phrase book falls portentously open. Practiced rummager of jumbled computer components in government surplus auctions, he reaches in and searches until he finds a compatible code. The flexibility of the extracted phrase pleases him, and he imagines various scenarios in which he might employ it.)

TOURIST   Here it is! – *sumimasen*, pardon me, are the shops open at this hour?

PEARL KING   Swift parachutes dropping
　　　　　　　sidelong through water,
　　　　　　　the octopus hordes come
　　　　　　　to rape the crop, shuck
　　　　　　　the mother oysters
　　　　　　　and swallow their flesh, spitting
　　　　　　　out pearls like melon seeds.
　　　　　　　Through smoky explosions of ink

the diving girls blindly
strike back with spears,
their white suits
stained with blue blood.

PART SECOND

(Heat raises a sweat from the sea; mist smudges landmarks from the
shore. The tourist rubs the vision like sleep from his eyes, staring about
in a state of appropriate startlement. He is in a museum, before a beach
diorama featuring a replica beach shelter. Within its straw walls a bored
woman wearing a starched white ensemble stands beside a firepit aflame
with orange plastic filaments. A statue of the Pearl King, regal in cape
and bowler, sceptre in hand, looks in through plate glass from its
courtyard pedestal with an expression of stern fortitude forever frozen
in bronze.)

TOURIST   What the...?

(Traces of seaweed cling nostalgically to his ankles. The unconsidered
possibility that he may himself be an exhibit lurks in the reptilian node
of his brain like an ominous rain cloud.)

DIVING GIRL   Thirty, forty, fifty, sixty
feet, as I grew taller
my descents deepened,
the reflection of a pine tree
lengthening across water.

(This should look good on her c.v. She's hoping to get another
television commercial soon, preferably one that doesn't involve laundry
products or paper diapers. Scotch whisky or pantyhose, perhaps.)

HOSTESS   Sir, may I direct you to the gift shop?

TOURIST   Where did they go, those people on the beach?

HOSTESS   The beach was replaced years ago with cement retaining walls. Why, you look like you've seen a ghost!

(Attuned to the distant frequency of elegantly modulated laughter, dolphins emit peacock-like mewls; polluted ocean currents carry their chortles away like lost sailors.)

DIVING GIRL   Always a girl
              I am made and unmade,
              each surfacing a birth,
              each dive a drowning,
              the whole world submerged and emerging
              again and again and again.

(She infuses the speech with a forceful emotion conjured by thoughts of her late hamster, Totoro.)

TOURIST   *Now I know the pearl*
              of the Buddha-nature
              Know its use:
              a boundless perfect sphere. [Han-Shan]

(Free of various theoretical prejudices pertaining to mimetic desire, he follows the hostess offstage, uttering for old time's sake an unrequited plaint to his mother, "but all the other kids have one!" Behind him, workers flick pearls into slotted black trays and deftly tally balanced sets of beads. The abacus of fortune softly clicks.)

II

NORTH ATLANTIC DRIFT

Baltasound

The horizon speaks the fluid blue
Equivocation of sky and sea.

The sound laps its long tongue inland
Past steatite heaped on the dock. Thimble of salt.

Parallels of stone. Harold Fairhair's road
Runs backward down the yellow hill.

A rabbit goes to ground. In mounds
The dead huddle together, hugging their knees.

The cairn spills. In this wish-hoard of rock
A thousand years old I anchor my stone.

North Atlantic Drift

My mother is a coastline
relying on rain and time,

and in a crofter's field the potatoes
beneath the brown loam,
harvested by hand when the green shaws wither,
boiled plain their flesh mealy, white
and good. My mother is

the soft blow soothing
the heather on the treeless slopes, sometimes
carrying the echoing steps of a girl
who footed all a Midsummer's Eve
through the roofless castle on the *voe*.
Nimble and watching always

with dark glancing eyes,
my mother is the collie running the sheep in
to shelter from the winter gale.

        ❧

I am not the rocky and constant coast
but a riptide where the Drift collides,
tempering the cold North Sea,

and I am the plankton floating in its stream,
shapeless like sand. I am

a neap tide
pulled by an uncharted moon,

lulled at the shore,

or a Selkie catching haddock in the harbour, sometimes
shedding my oily seadog pelt
to dance on land in human skin.

The Last Foal

In midsummer I carry my bag of turnip and peel
up the rocky slopes to where the stunted ponies graze,
grooming the green pelt of the *scattald*.
Shaggy yearlings rush for scraps, snorting
with fear and greed, their blunt teeth
brushing my palm. The one I want most,
a dusky old mare, avoids my outstretched hand.
She sways with her secret weight
away from the herd, the mottled orb
of her belly hanging close as a *hairst*
moon above the earth.

So near the pole. The season a slow glance
between the winds. On the shortest night
I sleep easily inside the cottage walls,
a warm quilt pillowing me
against the weather. As I dream the mare
makes her way in darkness up the withers of the hill
alone, to shelter in a stone dyke's
lee. In the quick black push
of night he arrives, trembling and wet.

It's late when I wake and take my cullings
up the hill. She's there,
resting in the sun while her new foal sleeps,
the other mares standing round him
silent as a ring of stones.
A young piebald lowers her head and
nips his clean white shoulder, as if checking

he's real. He shakes his heavy black head
and rises, his mother vigilant beneath her dark mane.

Later, after I've fed the horses,
the herd disperses and I toss the mare
the kale-heart I've saved for her,
but she turns away and crops across the shale,
wary and too wise to be tamed. The wind begins again,
biting through my coat and chafing my skin,
the day already many hours old.

Feeding Time

In the paddock
rams and wethers
run to the rattle of the pellet bucket,
all prattling and stammering
one muddy tongue
in voices ragged as winter fleece.

Nearby a new lamb practices
the same flat syllable, tasting,
over and over, its first
and only word,
a creamy curdled stutter
maybe *milk*, maybe *mother*.

The Ragman's Son

The ragman's son puts the pony in traces
while his father loads their wares:
homemade headache powder, thimbles and balloons,
a paper called *Neighbourly Wisdom*.
Peggy's iron-shod hooves ring out as the cart rolls
slowly through the city, unravelling lanes
where children run from doorways singing
The Ragman's coming! The Ragman's coming!

The children unpocket pennies for whistles
and the ragman's son stacks the wagon with scraps
their mothers bring to trade – shrunken sweaters,
skirts with worn seats, draperies faded with age.
He finds for himself a blackened pot of plenty
missing its lid. A cigarette lighter only
the flint of his eye will ignite, the good wool suit
of a soldier who won't be coming home.

When the ragman's cart grows heavy
he walks beside the pony with his son. They haul
metal to sell at the foundry, a box of bent spoons
and tin cans to be smelted into shillings.
Fabric, they sort into bales. Linen, cotton, wool.
At the cloth-mill the buyer sometimes
shorts them, paying calico prices
for a fine silk velvet, a rich bombazine.

At the end of the day the ragman packs
the pony's hooves with clay to draw the heat out.
The boy feels his own feet sore, growing too quickly
for his shoes. He likes cleaning Peggy's
beaded black feet, her relief as she leans
against his shoulder, her fetlock resting on his knee.

He scrapes loose the sea-rot smell,
a glass pebble that glitters like a gem.

The ragman's son digs deep, finds a diamond
stuck in her shoe, unmires old Roman coins
with heroes' worn faces, a monacle coated with muck.
With Neet's Foot he oils the cracked
bowls of her hooves, reaches farther into
his dream and draws out oranges, a crystal radio
crackling with song. An Airman's cap for his father
tumbles onto the stable floor, and a bolt
of embroidered satin for his mother.

After they've combed the city of every pin and spare
bit of string, in summer the ragman and his son
take a road that runs a grey worsted thread
through the country's loden shires.
The children working in the fields cry out
The Ragman's coming! The Ragman's coming!

While his father makes the fire the ragman's son
unharnesses Peggy and tethers her to graze
on wild grass. He spreads his blanket
under the cart, a temporary roof tilted on its axle
toward the stars. The boy stares up at the navy
serge of the sky, its scattered brass buttons,
falls asleep with deep blue lengths unfolding
forever in his eyes. The ground under,
and ahead of him, hard.

The Stillbirth

Dreaming a different life
my father moved us in the dead of winter
to an abandoned ranch he'd found
in the mountains. The summer before
he'd walked the welcoming land, conceived
a plan with almanacs and advice that flowed
free with the homemade wine of his neighbours,
bemused ranchers who wondered why a city man
would forfeit his salaried ease. He sat
with them on their evening porches, seeing
the gentle yellow order of the freshly swathed
fields, hearing the random
bleating of calves echo through the hills.

His children would flourish like the wild
alpine flowers that grew there
in spring. In summer he'd teach us
the names of grasses – *timothy, clover, oats, wheat.*
In winter we'd become strong
hauling hay and water, mucking stalls
in the old wooden barn.

That long January, as the eldest
I helped my father
feed the four Herefords. Our starter herd.
One morning in the early darkness
he found one of them had calved
too soon. He called me to the paddock
where the small body gleamed,

its upper side already leavening.
A smell like yeast rose from the salty
amniotic puddle it lay in.

It was perfect. Grotesque, hairless
except for white fringes on the shut
eyes, mouth and nostrils closed, hooves
still rubbery. Nearby the cow stood quietly
chewing the grain my father gave her, and
as he held her bucket he explained to me
gestation and its failures.

When he dropped me at the schoolbus
that morning my mouth was full of new words,
my ten year old's tongue morbidly savouring
the taste of things gone
wrong. I silently repeated their
magic – *stillborn, aborted, premature* –
as if they could convey the seamless
unfinished body and blue umbilicus
leaking into the frozen ground, the calf
first born of my father's dream.

Night Watch

The house groans as it sleeps,
its wooden bones creak. Within its
fitful ribs the family sleeps too.
Only the kitchen is awake and the girl
listening there alone, above the puff
of her own smoky breath
the fluorescent light's bored whine.
The oven is still faintly warm,
something to lean against, its intimate heat
like a hand on her back.
She sips her father's thin red wine
and hears the rest of the house sink
deeper into the dream, where children etch
hearts and curse words above their bunks
and their mother marks their growing
away from her in pencil on a door's
varnished frame.

                    Almost old enough
to know what night will tell her
the girl sees, beyond the violet
root bound on the windowsill,
the dark outside, foreign and deep.
In its temporary solitude
the fridge begins to hum. She feels
the house roll uneasily in its sleep,
hears the fretful timbre of its complaint
as it freights them all further toward light.

Island

Aspen branches uphold the wind as the worthiest cause,
Shake loose the last gusts like breath from a plastic bag.

In the art gallery the morning after the princess died
We cut up coloured paper to make postcards after Matisse.

A beach cabin waiting somewhere on a misty forested island.
A particular red rock riddled with white. A cube of raw meat.

The key will be hidden in the eaves, wrapped in crisp yellow
Leaves still smelling of linseed and turpentine.

This winter night and my reflection in the kitchen window
Polishing the rough, gathered stones of your laughter.

I signal you with smoke from heart made of wood
Too green to burn: *I wish you were here.*

III
THE ABACUS THAT COUNTS TIME

Mountain

Wild strawberries clustered on thin veins,
The mountain scarred with road.

Time arrives in a moth-white cloud. Gypsies.
The poplars shake their jade beads.

When to eat the heart of the thistle,
Where to find the giant footprint on a ledge.

For each answer a tariff: verglas, glaucous sap,
Lovers' names carved on the greenwood tree.

Hurt is a gift, a tender
Razor opening an emerald way in.

Canonic

The deal she struck herself, word wedded to deed,
the first clumsy attempt to streamline plot:
Tripped on the step – no, that's been done –
It happened opening the cupboard door:
the first thin story applied
like the poultices of salt her mother had made up
to blot wine spilled on the tablecloth,
as if cliché could soak up
the shock of the first blow. The initial lie
impressed on cheekbone with an onyx signet ring
and the long contract with fiction begun,

even years after the stories ended
still needing to remember
how she'd written them. And now,
as if taking the fabric from a drawer
to find the purple stain returned, she sees
the smudged impression has bloomed again,
a mildew beneath her eye. Like the mysterious
appearance of Mary's image on a bedroom wall,
that tale where the faithful travel long distances
to witness her weep real tears, how the lonely
man who'd tried to whitewash this wonder
now sits with believers in the rising damp
watching his plaster sweat.

What constitutes a miracle, what pilgrims
will she draw with the phenomenal
graffito of the flesh? This faint crescent
marking her skin, its dim blue moonlight barely
enough to read history by. The indelible smear
wax leaves when someone breaks the seal.

Black Labels

I've kept my look.
Women wanted me
then, and now. Am I to blame
wanting them too, sometimes? The wrong women
among the right, I didn't choose
carefully, some things you don't think about.
A few more Black Labels
and my face will start sagging
like his, my old man's the last time
I saw him. But my hand fits
this slim-waisted glass
so easy. Sometimes you don't give a damn.

I didn't, that raw morning
she came knocking on my window.
I crawled out of bed to let her in,
stood there shirtless, half-zipped,
nicotine and the night's leachate
of beer in my pores, her
stripping dirty sheets, picking up
empties and dumping ashtrays, just
like a mother, a step-mother, like any woman
come to straighten your life, making
the bed, then making me
into someplace easy to lie down in.
Just another woman,
a little worn. A little weird
to be screwing my father's
girlfriend.

I still have
his green eyes, the long nose, a little crooked

where he broke it. I press
the smooth-rimmed glass to
my lips. The lips she wanted,
they want still.

Black Plums

I'm getting buzzed on rum
I keep hidden from my wife
here in the dim shed.
Outside in the humming heat
the orchard branches sag –
engorged plums, fleshy peaches
round as a small child's bum.
The wasps getting drunk
on burst cherries.

From behind the wall
I hear my niece playing,
she wants to stroke
the soft feathers of the hens.
Nearly four, the girl still
sucks her thumb like a baby.
I call her in from the heat,
let her feel in my trouser pockets
for sweets.

I teach her to say
Little Jack Horner sat in a corner
eating his Christmas pie.
When she's finished her candy
and licked the juice from her chin,
I show her the trick
that always makes them giggle:
I tweak her nose and poke the nub
of my thumb between my fingers, saying
Oh, oh! What's this?
Who's got your nose?

She crows with excitement
and grabs at me with chubby hands.

It's time for her to learn
the rest of the rhyme:
He stuck in his thumb
and pulled out a plum.
Oh, I am all thumbs today.
I fumble around, pull out
the other candy and say
Look. What's this?
Its a treat for you.
Take it. Quick!

Now look what she's done.
I tuck myself away
and wipe off her sticky
fingers and face with a rag.
Before I send her out
I have her repeat
the game's final line
— *Oh, what a bad girl am I* –
until I'm satisfied
she's learned to play it
dumb.

Teeth

I

I got my first ring – plastic and paste – from a dentist after he drilled a tiny bicuspid. The taste of mercury's never left me.

Those baby teeth. Tenacious as barnacles, the way they hung on by their skin, not wanting to be traded in for a quarter left under the pillow. The way I hung on to the Tooth Fairy and Santa Claus long after they became implausible. Those first stubborn losses.

II

After the dentist pulled my first permanent molar, the hole healed over and something white started growing through the gum. I was beginning again, cutting a new tooth. But it was only broken root. A fragment of my former self.

That tooth was the first bead moved on the abacus that counts time. The first piece of the puzzle the missing Tooth Fairy is building, a little glow-in-the-dark dinosaur skeleton somewhere on the other side. Problem is, I'll have to relinquish the rest of me before she can put me together again.

At night while she's stockpiling parts I grind my teeth to a paste. Mortar and pestle of my worry, permanence wearing away.

III

They say you lose a tooth for every baby, each child leeching a little more of its mother. I say it's a tooth for every man, all

that love let down like milk. I finally figured this out when I
had all four wisdom teeth extracted in one sitting.

I know a guy whose eyetooth fell out shortly after his wife left
him, says he'd give the other to get her back. He refuses to
replace it, forsaking partial or implant, any false bridge to his
former smile. That black hole left for everyone to see, aching
to be filled.

Me, I prefer to keep my losses hidden, less incisive. Like the
half-forgotten hole my molar left. Just an empty space way
back in my head.

The ABC of Moles

Asymmetry. Border. Colour. The many brown eyes of an unearthed potato unblinking in the bathroom light, me in my moleskin suit making mountains, mapping the hollows and hills of myself, stroking the pale speckled egg of my body as if some secret is about to hatch. I read my skin's braille, join the dots with my finger to draw the full picture. Is something out of order? A beauty mark gone bad, trading its curves for a few rough edges and plotting to overthrow the body politic. Or deeper than that, a foreign agent who's infiltrated the border and gone underground for years, the trail of brown spots flagging his activity. A mole, so to speak. A Taupe or a Blue, burrowing blindly in the spongy cells, excavating dark mounds of dirt. The spoor I must track to some history hidden in the strata of my skin, beneath its dusty surface a rich loam full of bones. Under my fingers the irregular hue cries out, the random script, its simple letters, telling the tale of a stranger in a strange, strange land.

Burying the Shepherd

The rain winds down long enough
for him to wrap the dog
in an old quilt and lay her to rest
in the hole he's dug. Into it
he places a ball and a blue ribbon
from obedience school, a wedding snap
in which she sits beside the bride on the lawn.
In the photo she's a pup still,
black mask and muzzle
blurred against the creamy dress.

He shovels damp soil
and tamps the mound smooth,
a wound in the garden reminding him
of the illness the old dog slept finally
away. Now he has no one
to guide him into the dark
shelter of the past.

Out of some old loyalty
his ex-wife arrives, finds him
finishing up out back. The gate
stands open, its latch long broken,
the fence patched so often
against the dog's digging out
he'd given up trying to keep her in.

The woman awkwardly sets irises
on the grave, their long papery tongues
beginning to shrivel. A while since she
last saw the dog, she remembers it
barking at crows, the feel of warm fur
beneath her hand. Soon the earth will begin
to digest the body, eat the dark

frill from its lips, swallow
the vulva's black snail.
The lump of dirt pursed
like a mouth, everything she could say
now to comfort him is sealed
inside it. An image of grass
growing over the grave in spring,
the way a pearl smoothes over
a sharp thing, all she has
to offer, her own grief grown
thin from walking on it.

He feels something
stuck in him, a word
lodged in his throat like a bone.
When she leaves he stands
looking at the bleared winter sun,
sensing in its brief embrace
the weight of the rain's return, the stiff
body of the animal escaping,
already, into the ground.

String Of Pearls

String of beads, if you must break, break...
Princess Shikishi, d.1201

He wonders what she does the months
he's away, what other
life her letters may not mention,
the question in him a background
noise, an engine throbbing below deck.
He's sailing into a place where everything's submerged,
up past a chain of volcanic islands
through the Strait, beneath the polar sun
the tips of icebergs erupted like molars
on the sea's inscrutable face.

When the tanker enters its last empty port,
changing hands after anchoring in Nome,
he'll bring home the strand of pearls
she hinted she wanted in a letter.
This time he's coming from Japan,
carrying with him the shipyard's metal echo;
in his new camera a tourist's unfocused vision,
Fuji veiled in mist and wavering neon nights,
pictures that will tell her really
nothing of where he's been.

In Yokohama when he bought the pearls
he'd rubbed them against his teeth
to test their authenticity, their roughness
proving them real. One night in the pleasure-district
he'd watched a woman slip
a string of fakes large as quail eggs
deep inside her; another woman bent and took

the end between her lips, drew it out
slowly, silk from a dark sleeve. The beads broke
and spattered like hail on the wooden floor.

When he gets home he'll tell her
these pearls are properly knotted,
wanting to please her. He wonders if
she secretly wants something else,
what slips unknown through the dark
channels of a woman's life. Surprising,
how quickly pearls grow cold, the way the necklace
loses his heat when he isn't holding it.
When he gets home he'll tell her real pearls
must be worn on the skin to keep their sheen.

He can see how their milky surfaces
will lift into themselves the warmth of her body
in candlelight, gleam blue with the flame's
reflection. How perfectly matched they seem.
How perfectly his body will fit hers
when he gets home, all the ways
a woman can keep things hidden
sunk deep, unnamed. He'll put the rope of pearls
around her neck like a line thrown out for moorage,
anchor himself in her, bead by glistening bead.

Notes to The Pearl King

MERMAID

Mermaids assembled by Japanese fishermen from various animal parts were sold to travellers and exhibited in London and New York. Barnum's famous specimen was a hybrid of baby orangutan and salmon. To *girn* is to snarl or growl.

APPRENTICE

A dull pearl fed to a chicken would be recovered after sufficient time had passed for the bird's acidic gullet to buff away the pearl's outer layers, an ancient method of pearl doctoring described by Egyptian alchemists.

VEILED LOOKING GLASS

Louis Kornitzer coined some of these descriptive terms for pearls. *Shunga*, the erotic paintings and prints known as "spring pictures", were censored by edict in 1722. Tradition has it that master painter Kano Motonobu threw away his brush when attempting to portray Mt. Fudesute; *fudesute* means, "throwing away the brush."

THE SEA IS NOT CELIBATE

Flawed or undersized pearls are ground into calcium carbonate tablets for improving pregnancies, weak bones, and teeth. Pearls are also valued for aphrodisiac properties and restoring virility. Fresh viper's blood is another Japanese aphrodisiac. From some parts of Asia a copulating couple can be seen in the moon; from Japan, a rabbit pounding rice with a mortar and pestle is visible.

RED TIDE OR, *GYMNODINIUM MIKIMOTOI*

II Ago Bay is named for its shape, *ago* meaning "jaw" or "chin".

VI The complete curse may be found in *Exodus 7:14.*

VII The anger of the Dragon King of the Sea creates turbulent seas. In Japanese folklore, snakes often turn into swords, and vice versa. Many waterways are ruled by eels; when a nobleman tried to dump poison in the Tadami River in 1611, an eel appeared in the form of a monk and dissuaded him.

WATERBABY

A *mizugo*, or "waterbaby", is the spirit of a miscarried or aborted fetus; these spirits sometimes seek retribution for their premature deaths. The brother and sister divinities Izanagi and Izanami, creators of the islands of Japan, lost their first child to a miscarriage, and the boneless jellyfish-like being was put into the sea.

DREAM THIEF

Large, elongated ears are considered indicative of special gifts of insight and good fortune. In "the old story," a young village man eavesdrops as a lord's son tells his dream to the local dream reader, who predicts that the lord's son will become a powerful official. The young man persuades the dream reader to transfer the dream to him, by repeating it to her verbatim. The dream thief achieves his rise to power, while the original dreamer does not.

CHARM TO CONJURE PEARLS

A widely held belief found in records from the first century BC to the fifteenth AD, that pearls were formed by dew and coloured according to the weather, was questioned by Pliny the Second, who wondered how oysters at depths of twelve fathoms would be able to "inhale the quintessence of air." This practical impediment may explain why, when Columbus arrived in the West Indies, he recorded finding open-mouthed oysters hung on trees.

THE MURMURING OF THE SEA

The title is taken from a folktale which tells of an evil spirit who hears the sea chanting Buddha's teaching. The spirit follows the sound upriver to find that it originates in a brook that runs through a mountain monastery's privy.

DEAR HUSBAND: LETTER MAILED TO A REMOTE KELP FARM IN NORTHERN HOKKAIDO, NO RETURN ADDRESS

The poem's text is taken from a letter cited in Robert Eunson's biography of Mikimoto.

THE CRANE WIFE'S TALE

This is a variation on the traditional folktale. Ezra Pound's version of the Noh drama *Nishikigi* omits the following intriguing passage, which may be found in Donald Keene's translation, *The Brocade Tree:*

> Now, about the narrow cloth. Once there was in this place a bird of prey which carried off small children, to the intense grief of everybody. A rumor started that if the children were dressed in cloth woven of feathers, the bird would no longer take them. So the villagers wove the cloth to dress their children. At once, as predicted, the bird stopped seizing the children, and the cloth became much prized as a protective charm. But the cloth was narrow and its edges could not be joined; people wrote poems about lovers whose hearts could no more meet than the narrow cloth of Kefu in Michinoku.

GESTURE

The image comparing the puppeteer's face to an onion is Basho's, via Roland Barthes' essay on Bunraku theatre. Some passages from *The Love Suicides at Amijima* are quoted.

FACE

The last two lines of the poem are a variation on Basho's haiku.

UME

Ume means "plum" and is also a woman's name. Upon death, the deceased receives a new name, which is written in red on a small tablet, kept in the home.

THE CRANE WIFE'S TALE II

Married women once blackened their teeth with a compound of iron filings and plant gall extracts. A headdress that symbolically hides "horns of jealousy" is worn in traditional Japanese weddings. Long "swinging" sleeved kimono (*furisode*), is a style reserved for young women and brides, while women over 22, or married, wear "clipped wings" kimono (*tomesode*).

FROM THE PILLOW BOOK OF THE PEARL KING'S YOUNGEST DAUGHTER, "MEMORIES OF CERTAIN SPLENDID THINGS"

Mikimoto's replica of the Liberty Bell, displayed at the 1939 New York World's Fair, was covered in 12,250 pearls and 366 diamonds. His copy of Kyoto's five-storied Horyu Temple was studded with over 200,000 pearls. The italicised conversation is my paraphrase of an anonymous dialogue poem collected in *The Manyoshu*, an eighth century poetry anthology.

KAI AWASE: SHELL GAME II

A *kai awase* game chest was often part of an aristocratic woman's trousseau. A full set consisted of 360 pairs of clamshells, each pair painted with matching pictures inspired by literary or seasonal motifs. *Awase* means "matchings" or "joinings". To play, one at a time a "female" right-side (*degai*, or, "put-out" shell) is taken from the box and its mate sought amongst the "male" left-sides (*jigai*, or, "ground" shell) spread image-side down upon the floor.

The Jewel was one of three precious gifts the founder of China's T'ang dynasty sent to Japan after marrying a Japanese noblewoman. The Dragon King stole it enroute, and the bride's father asked a diver to retrieve it. She agreed on the condition that the nobleman name as sole heir the son he had fathered with her.

A possible inspiration for Japan's legendary Dragon King is the Giant Oarfish. These fish dwell on the abyssal plain at depths of 6,000 feet, and are rarely seen, as they surface only when dying. Up to 60 feet long, bluish silver, and with a red dorsal fin that runs the length of its flat body, the fish swims vertically, in a manner described as sword-like.

Notes to North Atlantic Drift

BALTASOUND

King Harold's Road, on Shetland's northernmost island of Unst, was built for the funeral procession of one of the ancient Norse warriors.

NORTH ATLANTIC DRIFT

A *voe* is an inlet or bay.

THE LAST FOAL

In the Shetland Islands a *scattald* is a tract of publicly owned grazing land. *Hairst* means "harvest".

Acknowledgements

Some of these poems have appeared in the following publications:
The Antigonish Review, Canadian Literature, The Dalhousie Review, Event, The Fiddlehead, Grain, Green Stone Mountain Review, The Malahat Review, The New Quarterly, The New Shetlander (UK), *Prairie Fire, Prism, Qwerty, Yomimono* (Japan), and the anthologies *Vintage 95* and *Chickweed: Sage Hill Poetry Series #1* (chapbook).

"Stillbirth" won first prize in the League of Canadian Poets' 1995 poetry contest.
"String of Pearls" won second prize in *Prairie Fire's* 1997 poetry contest.
"Nightwatch" won second prize in the Writers' Federation of New Brunswick's 2004 Literary Competition.
"*Kai Awase*: Shell Game II" won second prize in *The Antigonish Review's* 2003 "Great Blue Heron Poetry Competition", and is dedicated to Steve Noyes with love and appreciation.

My deepest thanks to everyone else who offered encouragement and ideas during the writing of these poems, with particular thanks to Robert Kroetsch, Liz Philips, and my editor at Brick Books, Don McKay. I'm grateful also to Stephen Gowman, Lorna Crozier, and Derk Wynand, who were there at the beginning. Special thanks to the gang: Scar, Pinstripe, Sugarlips, Dollface and Legs.

Thanks also to The Sage Hill Writing Experience and St. Peter's Abbey; The Banff Centre for the Arts; and The Canada Council for the Arts for financial assistance which made possible the book's completion.

Of many works consulted for the *Pearl King* sequence, *The Pearl King: The Story of the Fabulous Mikimoto* by Robert Eunson was an essential reference.

I'm indebted to Jim Greenwood for introducing me to the Mikimoto legend and for so generously sharing with me his passion for Japan; and to Anne Greenwood for old stories, Shetlandic wisdom, and her constant support. I appreciate also the hospitality of friends in Japan and Britain.

Finally, I'm much obliged to The Cat Sitters (especially the Sinclairs).

*C*atherine Greenwood
lives in Victoria on
Vancouver Island, not
far from her birthplace on the
49th parallel, Ladysmith, BC.
Her poetry has appeared
in various journals and
anthologies, and has won
several prizes, including the
2003 Bliss Carman Award.